THE ELEPHANT MAN

THE ELEPHANT MAN

A PLAY BY

Bernard Pomerance

GROVE PRESS, INC., NEW YORK

First Edition 1979
First Printing 1979
ISBN: 0–394–50642–1
Grove Press ISBN: 0–8021–0200–X
Library of Congress Catalog Card Number: 79–7792

First Evergreen Edition 1979
First Printing 1979
ISBN: 0–394–17539–5
Grove Press ISBN: 0–8021–4283–4
Library of Congress Catalog Card Number: 79–7792

Library of Congress Cataloging in Publication Data

Pomerance, Bernard.
  The elephant man.
  1. Merrick, John, 1862 or 3–1890—Drama. I. Title
PR6066.O48E4 1979   822'.9'14   79–7792
ISBN 0–394–50642–1
ISBN 0–394–17539–5 pbk.

Manufactured in the United States of America

Distributed by Random House, Inc., New York

GROVE PRESS, INC., 196 West Houston Street, New York, N.Y. 10014

Original cover art created and designed by Gil Lesser.

INTRODUCTORY NOTE

The Elephant Man was suggested by the life of John Merrick, known as The Elephant Man. It is recounted by Sir Frederick Treves in *The Elephant Man and Other Reminiscences,* Cassell and Co. Ltd., 1923. This account is reprinted in *The Elephant Man, A Study in Human Dignity,* by Ashley Montagu, Ballantine Books, 1973, to whom much credit is due for reviving contemporary interest in the story. My own knowledge of it came via my brother Michael, who told me the story, provided me with xeroxes of Treves' memoirs until I came on my own copy, and sent me the Montagu book. In Montagu's book are included photographs of Merrick as well as of Merrick's model of St. Phillip's Church. Merrick's bones are still at London Hospital.

I believe the building of the church model constitutes some kind of central metaphor, and the groping toward conditions where it can be built and the building of it are the action of the play. It does not, and should not, however, dominate the play visually, as I originally believed.

Merrick's face was so deformed he could not express any emotion at all. His speech was very difficult to understand without practice. Any attempt to reproduce his appearance and his speech naturalistically—*if* it were possible—would seem to me not only counterproductive, but, the more remarkably successful, the more distracting from the play. For how he appeared, let slide projections suffice.

If the pinheaded women are two actresses, then the play, in a pinch, can be performed with seven players, five men, two women.

THE ELEPHANT MAN

No one with any history of back trouble should attempt the part of MERRICK *as contorted. Anyone playing the part of* MERRICK *should be advised to consult a physician about the problems of sustaining any unnatural or twisted position.—B.P.*

The London production of *The Elephant Man* opened at the Hampstead Theatre, co-produced by the Hampstead Theatre and the Foco Novo Company, with the following cast:

CELLIST	Pat Arrowsmith
FREDERICK TREVES BELGIAN POLICEMAN	David Allister
CARR GOMM CONDUCTOR	William Hoyland
ROSS BISHOP WALSHAM HOW SNORK	Arthur Blake
JOHN MERRICK	David Schofield
PINHEAD NURSE SANDWICH PRINCESS ALEXANDRA DUCHESS JELLY WILLOW	Judy Bridgland
PINHEAD MRS. KENDAL COUNTESS	Jennie Stoller
PINHEAD MANAGER ENGLISH POLICEMAN PORTER LORD JOHN WILLOW	Ken Drury

This production was directed by Roland Rees; set and costumes by Tanya McCallin; costumes made and supervised by Lindy Hemming; lighting by Alan O'Toole; stage management by Clive Thacker, Neil Barnett, and Diana Goodman.

The Elephant Man was produced on Broadway at The Booth Theatre, on April 22, 1979, with the following cast:

FREDERICK TREVES BELGIAN POLICEMAN	Kevin Conway
CARR GOMM CONDUCTOR	Richard Clarke
ROSS BISHOP WALSHAM HOW SNORK	I. M. Hobson
JOHN MERRICK	Philip Anglim
PINHEAD MANAGER LONDON POLICEMAN WILL EARL LORD JOHN	John Neville-Andrews
PINHEAD MISS SANDWICH COUNTESS PRINCESS ALEXANDRA	Cordis Heard
MRS. KENDAL PINHEAD	Garole Shelley
ORDERLY	Dennis Creaghan
CELLIST	David Heiss

This production was directed by Jack Hofsiss; set by David Jenkins; costumes by Julie Weiss; lighting by Beverly Emmons; produced by Richmond Crinkley, Elizabeth I. McCann, and Nelle Nugent; Ray Larsen and Ted Snowden, associate producers.

1884–1890. London. One scene is in Belgium.

CHARACTERS

FREDERICK TREVES, a surgeon and teacher

CARR GOMM, administrator of the London Hospital

ROSS, Manager of the Elephant Man

JOHN MERRICK, the Elephant Man

Three PINHEADS, three women freaks whose heads are
pointed

BELGIAN POLICEMAN

LONDON POLICEMAN

MAN, at a fairground in Brussels

CONDUCTOR, of Ostend-London boat train

BISHOP WALSHAM HOW

PORTER, at the London Hospital

SNORK, also a porter

MRS. KENDAL, an actress

DUCHESS

COUNTESS

PRINCESS ALEXANDRA

LORD JOHN

NURSE, MISS SANDWICH

SCENE I

HE WILL HAVE 100 GUINEA FEES BEFORE HE'S FORTY

The London Hospital, Whitechapel Rd. Enter GOMM, *enter* TREVES.

TREVES: Mr. Carr Gomm? Frederick Treves. Your new lecturer in anatomy.

GOMM: Age thirty-one. Books on Scrofula and Applied Surgical Anatomy—I'm happy to see you rising, Mr. Treves. I like to see merit credited, and your industry, accomplishment, and skill all do you credit. Ignore the squalor of Whitechapel, the general dinginess, neglect and poverty without, and you will find a continual medical richesse in the London Hospital. We study and treat the widest range of diseases and disorders, and are certainly the greatest institution of our kind in the world. The Empire provides unparalleled opportunities for our studies, as places cruel to life are the most revealing scientifically. Add to our reputation by going further, and that'll satisfy. You've bought a house?

TREVES: On Wimpole Street.

1

GOMM: Good. Keep at it, Treves. You'll have an FRS and 100 guinea fees before you're forty. You'll find it is an excellent consolation prize.

TREVES: Consolation? I don't know what you mean.

GOMM: I know you don't. You will. (*Exits.*)

TREVES: A happy childhood in Dorset.
　　　　A scientist in an age of science.
　　　　In an English age, an Englishman. A teacher and a doctor at the London. Two books published by my thirty-first year. A house. A wife who loves me, and my god, 100 guinea fees before I'm forty.
　　　　Consolation for what?
　　　　As of the year AD 1884, I, Freddie Treves, have excessive blessings. Or so it seems to me.

Blackout.

SCENE II

------∞------

ART IS AS NOTHING TO NATURE

Whitechapel Rd. A storefront. A large advertisement of a creature with an elephant's head. ROSS, *his manager.*

ROSS: Tuppence only, step in and see: This side of the grave, John Merrick has no hope nor expectation of relief. In every sense his situation is desperate. His physical agony is exceeded only by his mental anguish, a despised creature without consolation. Tuppence only, step in and see! To live with his physical hideousness, incapacitating deformities and unremitting pain is trial enough, but to be exposed to the cruelly lacerating expressions of horror and disgust by all who behold him—is even more difficult to bear. Tuppence only, step in and see! For in order to survive, Merrick forces himself to suffer these humiliations, I repeat, humiliations, in order to survive, thus he exposes himself to crowds who pay to gape and yawp at this freak of nature, the Elephant Man.

Enter TREVES *who looks at advertisement.*

ROSS: See Mother Nature uncorseted and in malignant rage! Tuppence.

TREVES: This sign's absurd. Half-elephant, half-man is not possible. Is he foreign?

ROSS: Right, from Leicester. But nothing to fear.

TREVES: I'm at the London across the road. I would be curious to see him if there is some genuine disorder. If he is a mass of papier-maché and paint however—

ROSS: Then pay me nothing. Enter, sir. Merrick, stand up. Ya bloody donkey, up, up.

They go in, then emerge. TREVES *pays.*

TREVES: I must examine him further at the hospital. Here is my card. I'm Treves. I will have a cab pick him up and return him. My card will gain him admittance.

ROSS: Five bob he's yours for the day.

TREVES: I wish to examine him in the interests of science, you see.

ROSS: Sir, I'm Ross. I look out for him, get him his living. Found him in Leicester workhouse. His own ma put him there age of three. Couldn't bear the sight, well you can see why. We—he and I—are in business. He is our capital, see. Go to a bank. Go anywhere. Want to borrow capital, you pay interest. Scientists even. He's good value though. You won't find another like him.

TREVES: Fair enough. (*He pays.*)

ROSS: Right. Out here, Merrick. Ya bloody donkey, out!

Lights fade out.

4

SCENE III

WHO HAS SEEN THE LIKE OF THIS?

TREVES *lectures.* MERRICK *contorts himself to approximate projected slides of the real Merrick.*

TREVES: The most striking feature about him was his enormous head. Its circumference was about that of a man's waist. From the brow there projected a huge bony mass like a loaf, while from the back of his head hung a bag of spongy fungous-looking skin, the surface of which was comparable to brown cauliflower. On the top of the skull were a few long lank hairs. The osseous growth on the forehead, at this stage about the size of a tangerine, almost occluded one eye. From the upper jaw there projected another mass of bone. It protruded from the mouth like a pink stump, turning the upper lip inside out, and making the mouth a wide slobbering aperture. The nose was merely a lump of flesh, only recognizable as a nose from its position. The deformities rendered the face utterly incapable of the expression of any emotion whatsoever. The back was horrible because from it hung,

5

as far down as the middle of the thigh, huge sack-like masses of flesh covered by the same loathsome cauliflower stain. The right arm was of enormous size and shapeless. It suggested but was not elephantiasis, and was overgrown also with pendant masses of the same cauliflower-like skin. The right hand was large and clumsy—a fin or paddle rather than a hand. No distinction existed between the palm and back, the thumb was like a radish, the fingers like thick tuberous roots. As a limb it was useless. The other arm was remarkable by contrast. It was not only normal, but was moreover a delicately shaped limb covered with a fine skin and provided with a beautiful hand which any woman might have envied. From the chest hung a bag of the same repulsive flesh. It was like a dewlap suspended from the neck of a lizard. The lower limbs had the characters of the deformed arm. They were unwieldy, dropsical-looking, and grossly misshapen. There arose from the fungous skin growths a very sickening stench which was hard to tolerate. To add a further burden to his trouble, the wretched man when a boy developed hip disease which left him permanently lame, so that he could only walk with a stick. *(To* MERRICK*)* Please. (MERRICK *walks.)* He was thus denied all means of escape from his tormentors.

VOICE: Mr. Treves, you have shown a profound and unknown disorder to us. You have said when he leaves here it is for his exhibition again. I do not think it ought to be permitted. It is a disgrace. It is a pity and a disgrace. It is an indecency in fact. It may be a danger in ways we do not know. Something ought to be done about it.

TREVES: I am a doctor. What would you have me do?

VOICE: Well. I know what to do. *I* know.

Silence. A policeman enters as lights fade out.

SCENE IV

THIS INDECENCY MAY NOT
CONTINUE

Music. A fair. PINHEADS *huddling together, holding
a portrait of Leopold, King of the Congo. Enter* MAN.

MAN: Now, my pinheaded darlings, your attention please.
Every freak in Brussels Fair is doing something to
celebrate Leopold's fifth year as King of the Congo.
Him. Our King. Our Empire. *(They begin reciting.)*
No, don't recite yet, you morons. I'll say when. And
when you do, get it *right.* You don't, it's back to the
asylum. Know what that means, don't you? They'll cut
your heads. They'll spoon out your little brains, re-
place 'em in the dachshund they were nicked from.
Cut you. Yeah. Be back with customers. Come see the
Queens of the Congo! *(Exits.)*

Enter MERRICK, ROSS.

MERRICK: Cosmos? Cosmos?

ROSS: Congo. Land of darkness. Hoho! *(Sees* PINS.*)* Look
at them, lad. It's freer on the continent. Loads of indecency here, no one minds. You won't get coppers sent

8

round to roust you out like London. Reckon in Brussels here's our fortune. You have a little tête-à-tête with this lot while I see the coppers about our license to exhibit. Be right back. *(Exits.)*

MERRICK: I come from England.

PINS: Allo!

MERRICK: At home they chased us. Out of London. Police. Someone complained. They beat me. You have no trouble? No?

PINS: Allo! Allo!

MERRICK: Hello. In Belgium we make money. I look forward to it. Happiness, I mean. You pay your police? How is it done?

PINS: Allo! Allo!

MERRICK: We do a show together sometime? Yes? I have saved forty-eight pounds. Two shillings. Nine pence. English money. Ross takes care of it.

PINS: Allo! Allo!

MERRICK: Little vocabulary problem, eh? Poor things. Looks like they put your noses to the grindstone and forgot to take them away.

MAN *enters*.

MAN: They're coming.

(People enter to see the girls' act.)

Now.

PINS *(dancing and singing)*:

9

We are the Queens of the Congo,
The Beautiful Belgian Empire
Our niggers are bigger
Our miners are finer
Empire, Empire, Congo and power
Civilizuzu's finest hour
Admire, perspire, desire, acquire
Or we'll set you on fire!

MAN: You cretins! Sorry, they're not ready yet. Out please.

(People exit.)

Get those words right, girls! Or you know what.

MAN *exits.* PINS *weep.*

MERRICK: Don't cry. You sang nicely. Don't cry. There there.

Enter ROSS *in grip of two* POLICEMEN.

ROSS: I was promised a permit. I lined a tour up on that!

POLICEMEN: This is a brutal, indecent, and immoral display. It is a public indecency, and it is forbidden here.

ROSS: What about them with their perfect cone heads?

POLICEMEN: They are ours.

ROSS: Competition's good for business. Where's your spirit of competition?

POLICEMEN: Right here. *(Smacks* MERRICK.*)*

ROSS: Don't do that, you'll kill him!

POLICEMEN: Be better off dead. Indecent bastard.

MERRICK: Don't cry girls. Doesn't hurt.

PINS: Indecent, indecent, indecent, indecent!!

POLICEMEN escort MERRICK *and* ROSS *out, i.e., forward. Blackout except spot on* MERRICK *and* ROSS.

MERRICK: Ostend will always mean bad memories. Won't it, Ross?

ROSS: I've decided. I'm sending you back, lad. You're a flop. No, you're a liability. You ain't the moneymaker I figured, so that's it.

MERRICK: Alone?

ROSS: Here's a few bob, have a nosh. I'm keeping the rest. For my trouble. I deserve it, I reckon. Invested enough with you. Pick up your stink if I stick around. Stink of failure. Stink of lost years. Just stink, stink, stink, stink, stink.

Enter CONDUCTOR.

CONDUCTOR: This the one?

ROSS: Just see him to Liverpool St. Station safe, will you? Here's for your trouble.

MERRICK: Robbed.

CONDUCTOR: What's he say?

ROSS: Just makes sounds. Fella's an imbecile.

MERRICK: Robbed.

ROSS: Bon voyage, Johnny. His name is Johnny. He knows his name, that's all, though.

11

CONDUCTOR: Don't follow him, Johnny. Johnny, come on boat now. Conductor find Johnny place out of sight. Johnny! Johnny! Don't struggle, Johnny. Johnny come on.

MERRICK: Robbed! Robbed!

Fadeout on struggle.

SCENE V

POLICE SIDE WITH IMBECILE AGAINST THE CROWD

Darkness. Uproar, shouts.

VOICE: Liverpool St. Station!

Enter MERRICK, CONDUCTOR, POLICEMAN.

POLICEMAN: We're safe in here. I barred the door.

CONDUCTOR: They wanted to rip him to pieces. I've never seen anything like it. It was like being Gordon at bleedin' Khartoum.

POLICEMAN: Got somewhere to go in London, lad? Can't stay here.

CONDUCTOR: He's an imbecile. He don't understand. Search him.

POLICEMAN: Got any money?

MERRICK: Robbed.

POLICEMAN: What's that?

13

CONDUCTOR: He just makes sounds. Frightened sounds is all he makes. Go through his coat.

MERRICK: Je-sus.

POLICEMAN: Don't let me go through your coat, I'll turn you over to that lot! Oh, I was joking, don't upset yourself.

MERRICK: Joke? Joke?

POLICEMAN: Sure, croak, croak, croak, croak.

MERRICK: Je-sus.

POLICEMAN: Got a card here. You Johnny Merrick? What's this old card here, Johnny? Someone give you a card?

CONDUCTOR: What's it say?

POLICEMAN: Says Mr. Frederick Treves, Lecturer in Anatomy, the London Hospital.

CONDUCTOR: I'll go see if I can find him, it's not far. *(Exits.)*

POLICEMAN: What's he do, lecture you on your anatomy? People who think right don't look like that then, do they? Yeah, glung glung, glung, glung.

MERRICK: Jesus. Jesus.

POLICEMAN: Sure, Treves, Treves, Treves, Treves.

Blackout, then lights go up as CONDUCTOR *leads* TREVES *in.*

TREVES: What is going on here? Look at that mob, have you no sense of decency. I am Frederick Treves. This is my card.

POLICEMAN: This poor wretch here had it. Arrived from Ostend.

TREVES: Good Lord, Merrick? John Merrick? What has happened to you?

MERRICK: Help me!

Fadeout.

SCENE VI

EVEN ON THE NIGER AND CEYLON, NOT THIS

The London Hospital. MERRICK *in bathtub.* TREVES *outside. Enter* MISS SANDWICH.

TREVES: You are? Miss Sandwich?

SANDWICH: Sandwich. Yes.

TREVES: You have had experience in missionary hospitals in the Niger.

SANDWICH: And Ceylon.

TREVES: I may assume you've seen—

SANDWICH: The tropics. Oh those diseases. The many and the awful scourges our Lord sends, yes, sir.

TREVES: I need the help of an experienced nurse, you see.

SANDWICH: Someone to bring him food, take care of the room. Yes, I understand. But it is somehow difficult.

TREVES: Well, I have been let down so far. He really is— that is, the regular sisters—well, it is not part of their job and they will not do it. Be ordinarily kind to Mr. Merrick. Without—well—panicking. He is quite beyond ugly. You understand that? His appearance has terrified them.

SANDWICH: The photographs show a terrible disease.

TREVES: It is a disorder, not a disease; it is in no way contagious though we don't in fact know what it is. I have found however that there is a deep superstition in those I've tried, they actually believe he somehow brought it on himself, this thing, and of course it is not that at all.

SANDWICH: I am not one who believes it is ourselves who attain grace or bring chastisement to us, sir.

TREVES: Miss Sandwich, I am hoping not.

SANDWICH: Let me put your mind to rest. Care for lepers in the East, and you have cared, Mr. Treves. In Africa, I have seen dreadful scourges quite unknown to our more civilized climes. What at home could be worse than a miserable and afflicted rotting black?

TREVES: I imagine.

SANDWICH: Appearances do not daunt me.

TREVES: It is really that that has sent me outside the confines of the London seeking help.

SANDWICH: "I look unto the hills whence cometh my help." I understand: I think I will be satisfactory.

Enter PORTER *with tray*.

PORTER: His lunch. *(Exits.)*

TREVES: Perhaps you would be so kind as to accompany me this time. I will introduce you.

17

SANDWICH: Allow me to carry the tray.

TREVES: I will this time. You are ready.

SANDWICH: I am.

TREVES: He is bathing to be rid of his odor.

(*They enter to* MERRICK.)

John, this is Miss Sandwich. She—

SANDWICH: I—(*unable to control herself*) Oh my good God in heaven. (*Bolts room.*)

TREVES (*puts* MERRICK's *lunch down*): I am sorry. I thought—

MERRICK: Thank you for saving the lunch this time.

TREVES: Excuse me.

(*Exits to* MISS SANDWICH.)

You have let me down, you know. I did everything to warn you and still you let me down.

SANDWICH: You didn't say.

TREVES: But I—

SANDWICH: Didn't! You said—just words!

TREVES: But the photographs.

SANDWICH: Just pictures. No one will do this. I am sorry. (*Exits.*)

TREVES: Yes. Well. This is not helping him.

Fadeout.

SCENE VII

THE ENGLISH PUBLIC WILL PAY FOR HIM TO BE LIKE US

The London Hospital. MERRICK *in a bathtub reading.* TREVES, BISHOP HOW *in foreground.*

BISHOP: With what fortitude he bears his cross! It is remarkable. He has made the acquaintance of religion and knows sections of the Bible by heart. Once I'd grasped his speech, it became clear he'd certainly had religious instruction at one time.

TREVES: I believe it was in the workhouse, Dr. How.

BISHOP: They are awfully good about that sometimes. The psalms he loves, and the book of Job perplexes him, he says, for he cannot see that a just God must cause suffering, as he puts it, merely then to be merciful. Yet that Christ will save him he does not doubt, so he is not resentful.

Enter GOMM.

GOMM: Christ had better; be damned if we can.

BISHOP: Ahem. In any case Dr. Treves, he has a religious

19

nature, further instruction would uplift him and I'd be pleased to provide it. I plan to speak of him from the pulpit this week.

GOMM: I see our visiting bather has flushed the busy Bishop How from his cruciform lair.

BISHOP: Speak with Merrick, sir. I have spoken to him of Mercy and Justice. There's a true Christian in the rough.

GOMM: This makes my news seem banal, yet yes: Frederick, the response to my letter to the *Times* about Merrick has been staggering. The English public has been so generous that Merrick may be supported for life without a penny spent from Hospital funds.

TREVES: But that is excellent.

BISHOP: God bless the English public.

GOMM: Especially for not dismembering him at Liverpool St. Station. Freddie, the London's no home for incurables, this is quite irregular, but for you I permit it— though god knows what you'll do.

BISHOP: God does know, sir, and Darwin does not.

GOMM: He'd better, sir; he deformed him.

BISHOP: I had apprehensions coming here. I find it most fortunate Merrick is in the hands of Dr. Treves, a Christian, sir.

GOMM: Freddie is a good man and a brilliant doctor, and that is fortunate indeed.

TREVES: I couldn't have raised the funds though, Doctor.

BISHOP: Don't let me keep you longer from your duties, Mr. Treves. Yet, Mr. Gomm, consider: is it science, sir, that motivates us when we transport English rule of law to India or Ireland? When good British churchmen leave hearth and home for missionary hardship in Africa, is it science that bears them away? Sir it is not. It is Christian duty. It is the obligation to bring our light and benefices to benighted man. That motivates us, even as it motivates Treves toward Merrick, sir, to bring salvation where none is. Gordon was a Christian, sir, and died at Khartoum for it. Not for science, sir.

GOMM: You're telling me, not for science.

BISHOP: Mr. Treves, I'll visit Merrick weekly if I may.

TREVES: You will be welcome, sir, I am certain.

BISHOP: Then good day, sirs. (*Exits.*)

GOMM: Well, Jesus my boy, now we have the money, what do you plan for Merrick?

TREVES: Normality as far as is possible.

GOMM: So he will be like us? Ah. (*Smiles.*)

TREVES: Is something wrong, Mr. Gomm? With us?

Fadeout.

SCENE VIII

MERCY AND JUSTICE ELUDE
OUR MINDS AND ACTIONS

MERRICK *in bath*. TREVES, GOMM.

MERRICK: How long is as long as I like?

TREVES: You may stay for life. The funds exist.

MERRICK: Been reading this. About homes for the blind.
Wouldn't mind going to one when I have to move.

TREVES: But you do not have to move; and you're not
blind.

MERRICK: I would prefer it where no one stared at me.

GOMM: No one will bother you here.

TREVES: Certainly not. I've given instructions.

PORTER *and* SNORK *peek in*.

PORTER: What'd I tell you?

SNORK: Gawd almighty. Oh. Mr. Treves. Mr. Gomm.

TREVES: You were told not to do this. I don't understand.
You must not lurk about. Surely you have work.

PORTER: Yes, sir.

TREVES: Well, it is infuriating. When you are told a thing, you must listen. I won't have you gaping in on my patients. Kindly remember that.

PORTER: Isn't a patient, sir, is he?

TREVES: Do not let me find you here again.

PORTER: Didn't know you were here, sir. We'll be off now.

GOMM: No, no, Will. Mr. Treves was precisely saying no one would intrude when you intruded.

TREVES: He is warned now. Merrick does not like it.

GOMM: He was warned before. On what penalty, Will?

PORTER: That you'd sack me, sir.

GOMM: You are sacked, Will. You, his friend, you work here?

SNORK: Just started last week, sir.

GOMM: Well, I hope the point is taken now.

PORTER: Mr. Gomm—I ain't truly sacked, am I?

GOMM: Will, yes. Truly sacked. You will never be more truly sacked.

PORTER: It's not me. My wife ain't well. My sister has got to take care of our kids, and of her. Well.

GOMM: Think of them first next time.

PORTER: It ain't as if I interfered with his medicine.

GOMM: That is exactly what it is. You may go.

PORTER: Just keeping him to look at in private. That's all. Isn't it?

SNORK *and* PORTER *exit*.

GOMM: There are priorities, Frederick. The first is discipline. Smooth is the passage to the tight ship's master. Merrick, you are safe from prying now.

TREVES: Have we nothing to say, John?

MERRICK: If all that'd stared at me'd been sacked—there'd be whole towns out of work.

TREVES: I meant, "Thank you, sir."

MERRICK: "Thank you sir."

TREVES: We always do say please and thank you, don't we?

MERRICK: Yes, sir. Thank you.

TREVES: If we want to properly be like others.

MERRICK: Yes, sir, I want to.

TREVES: Then it is for our own good, is it not?

MERRICK: Yes, sir. Thank you, Mr. Gomm.

GOMM: Sir, you are welcome. (*Exits.*)

TREVES: You are happy here, are you not, John?

MERRICK: Yes.

TREVES: The baths have rid you of the odor, have they not?

MERRICK: First chance I had to bathe regular. Ly.

TREVES: And three meals a day delivered to your room?

MERRICK: Yes, sir.

TREVES: This is your Promised Land, is it not? A roof. Food. Protection. Care. Is it not?

MERRICK: Right, Mr. Treves.

TREVES: I will bet you don't know what to call this.

MERRICK: No, sir, I don't know.

TREVES: You call it, Home.

MERRICK: Never had a home before.

TREVES: You have one now. Say it, John: Home.

MERRICK: Home.

TREVES: No, no, really say it. I have a home. This is my. Go on.

MERRICK: I have a home. This is my home. This is my home. I have a home. As long as I like?

TREVES: That is what home is.

MERRICK: That is what is home.

TREVES: If I abide by the rules, I will be happy.

MERRICK: Yes, sir.

TREVES: Don't be shy.

MERRICK: If I abide by the rules I will be happy.

TREVES: Very good. Why?

MERRICK: Why what?

TREVES: Will you be happy?

MERRICK: Because it is my home?

TREVES: No, no. Why do rules make you happy?

MERRICK: I don't know.

TREVES: Of course you do.

MERRICK: No, I really don't.

TREVES: Why does anything make you happy?

MERRICK: Like what? Like what?

TREVES: Don't be upset. Rules make us happy because they are for our own good.

MERRICK: Okay.

TREVES: Don't be shy, John. You can say it.

MERRICK: This is my home?

TREVES: No. About rules making us happy.

MERRICK: They make us happy because they are for our own good.

TREVES: Excellent. Now: I am submitting a follow-up paper on you to the London Pathological Society. It would help if you told me what you recall about your first years, John. To fill in gaps.

MERRICK: To fill in gaps. The workhouse where they put me. They beat you there like a drum. Boom boom: scrape the floor white. Shine the pan, boom boom. It never ends. The floor is always dirty. The pan is always tarnished. There is nothing you can do about it. You are always attacked anyway. Boom boom. Boom boom. Boom boom. Will the children go to the work-house?

TREVES: What children?

MERRICK: The children. The man he sacked.

TREVES: Of necessity Will will find other employment. You don't want crowds staring at you, do you?

MERRICK: No.

TREVES: In your own home you do not have to have crowds staring at you. Or anyone. Do you? In your home?

MERRICK: No.

TREVES: Then Mr. Gomm was merciful. You yourself are proof. Is it not so? *(Pause.)* Well? Is it not so?

MERRICK: If your mercy is so cruel, what do you have for justice?

TREVES: I am sorry. It is just the way things are.

MERRICK: Boom boom. Boom boom. Boom boom.

Fadeout.

SCENE IX

MOST IMPORTANT ARE WOMEN

MERRICK *asleep, head on knees.* TREVES, MRS. KENDAL *foreground.*

TREVES: You have seen photographs of John Merrick, Mrs. Kendal. You are acquainted with his appearance.

MRS. KENDAL: He reminds me of an audience I played Cleopatra for in Brighton once. All huge grim head and grimace and utterly unable to clap.

TREVES: Well. My aim's to lead him to as normal a life as possible. His terror of us all comes from having been held at arm's length from society. I am determined that shall end. For example, he loves to meet people and converse. I am determined he shall. For example, he had never seen the inside of any normal home before. I had him to mine, and what a reward, Mrs. Kendal; his astonishment, his joy at the most ordinary things. Most critical I feel, however, are women. I will explain. They have always shown the greatest fear and loathing of him. While he adores them of course.

MRS. KENDAL: Ah. He is intelligent.

TREVES: I am convinced they are the key to retrieving him from his exclusion. Though, I must warn you, women are not quite real to him—more creatures of his imagination.

MRS. KENDAL: Then he is already like other men, Mr. Treves.

TREVES: So I thought, an actress could help. I mean, unlike most women, you won't give in, you are trained to hide your true feelings and assume others.

MRS. KENDAL: You mean unlike most women I am famous for it, that is really all.

TREVES: Well. In any case. If you could enter the room and smile and wish him good morning. And when you leave, shake his hand, the left one is usable, and really quite beautiful, and say, "I am very pleased to have made your acquaintance, Mr. Merrick."

MRS. KENDAL: Shall we try it? Left hand out please. *(Suddenly radiant)* I am *very* pleased to have made your acquaintance Mr. Merrick. I am very *pleased* to have made your acquaintance Mr. Merrick. I am very pleased to have made your *acquaintance* Mr. Merrick. I *am* very pleased to have made *your* acquaintance Mr. Merrick. Yes. That one.

TREVES: By god, they are all splendid. Merrick will be so pleased. It will be the day he becomes a man like other men.

MRS. KENDAL: Speaking of that, Mr. Treves.

TREVES: Frederick, please.

MRS. KENDAL: Freddie, may I commit an indiscretion?

TREVES: Yes?

MRS. KENDAL: I could not but help noticing from the photographs that—well—of the unafflicted parts—ah, how shall I put it? *(Points to photograph.)*

TREVES: Oh. I see! I quite. Understand. No, no, no, it is quite normal.

MRS. KENDAL: I thought as much.

TREVES: Medically speaking, uhm, you see the papillomatous extrusions which disfigure him, uhm, seem to correspond quite regularly to the osseous deformities, that is, excuse me, there is a link between the bone disorder and the skin growths, though for the life of me I have not discovered what it is or why it is, but in any case this—part—it would be therefore unlikely to be afflicted because well, that is, well, there's no bone in it. None at all. I mean.

MRS. KENDAL: Well. Learn a little every day don't we?

TREVES: I am horribly embarrassed.

MRS. KENDAL: Are you? Then he must be lonely indeed.

Fadeout.

SCENE X

━━━━━∽━━━━━

WHEN THE ILLUSION ENDS HE
MUST KILL HIMSELF

MERRICK *sketching. Enter* TREVES, MRS. KENDAL.

TREVES: He is making sketches for a model of St. Phillip's church. He wants someday to make a model, you see. John, my boy, this is Mrs. Kendal. She would very much like to make your acquaintance.

MRS. KENDAL: Good morning Mr. Merrick.

TREVES: I will see to a few matters. I will be back soon. (*Exits.*)

MERRICK: I planned so many things to say. I forget them. You are so beautiful.

MRS. KENDAL: How charming, Mr. Merrick.

MERRICK: Well. Really that was what I planned to say. That I forgot what I planned to say. I couldn't think of anything else I was so excited.

MRS. KENDAL: Real charm is always planned, don't you think?

MERRICK: Well. I do not know why I look like this, Mrs. Kendal. My mother was so beautiful. She was knocked down by an elephant in a circus while she was pregnant. Something must have happened, don't you think?

MRS. KENDAL: It may well have.

MERRICK: It may well have. But sometimes I think my head is so big because it is so full of dreams. Because it is. Do you know what happens when dreams cannot get out?

MRS. KENDAL: Why, no.

MERRICK: I don't either. Something must. *(Silence.)* Well. You are a famous actress.

MRS. KENDAL: I am not unknown.

MERRICK: You must display yourself for your living then. Like I did.

MRS. KENDAL: That is not myself, Mr. Merrick. That is an illusion. This is myself.

MERRICK: This is myself too.

MRS. KENDAL: Frederick says you like to read. So: books.

MERRICK: I am reading *Romeo and Juliet* now.

MRS. KENDAL: Ah. Juliet. What a love story. I adore love stories.

MERRICK: I like love stories best too. If I had been Romeo, guess what.

MRS. KENDAL: What?

32

MERRICK: I would not have held the mirror to her breath.

MRS. KENDAL: You mean the scene where Juliet appears to be dead and he holds a mirror to her breath and sees—

MERRICK: Nothing. How does it feel when he kills himself because he just sees nothing?

MRS. KENDAL: Well. My experience as Juliet has been— particularly with an actor I will not name—that while I'm laying there dead dead dead, and he is lamenting excessively, I get to thinking that if this slab of ham does not part from the hamhock of his life toute suite, I am going to scream, pop off the tomb, and plunge a dagger into his scene-stealing heart. Romeos are very undependable.

MERRICK: Because he does not care for Juliet.

MRS. KENDAL: Not care?

MERRICK: Does he take her pulse? Does he get a doctor? Does he make sure? No. He kills himself. The illusion fools him because he does not care for her. He only cares about himself. If I had been Romeo, we would have got away.

MRS. KENDAL: But then there would be no play, Mr. Merrick.

MERRICK: If he did not love her, why should there be a play? Looking in a mirror and seeing nothing. That is not love. It was all an illusion. When the illusion ended he had to kill himself.

MRS. KENDAL: Why. That is extraordinary.

MERRICK: Before I spoke with people, I did not think of all these things because there was no one to bother to think them for. Now things just come out of my mouth which are true.

TREVES *enters.*

TREVES: You are famous, John. We are in the papers. Look. They have written up my report to the Pathological Society. Look—it is a kind of apotheosis for you.

MRS. KENDAL: Frederick, I feel Mr. Merrick would benefit by even more company than you provide; in fact by being acquainted with the best, and they with him. I shall make it my task if you'll permit. As you know, I am a friend of nearly everyone, and I do pretty well as I please and what pleases me is this task, I think.

TREVES: By god, Mrs. Kendal, you are splendid.

MRS. KENDAL: Mr. Merrick I must go now. I should like to return if I may. And so that we may without delay teach you about society, I would like to bring my good friend Dorothy Lady Neville. She would be most pleased if she could meet you. Let me tell her yes?

(MERRICK *nods yes.*)

Then until next time. I'm sure your church model will surprise us all. Mr. Merrick, it has been a very great pleasure to make your acquaintance.

TREVES: John. Your hand. She wishes to shake your hand.

MERRICK: Thank you for coming.

34

MRS. KENDAL: But it was my pleasure. Thank you. *(Exits, accompanied by* TREVES.*)*

TREVES: What a wonderful success. Do you know he's never shook a woman's hand before?

As lights fade MERRICK *sobs soundlessly, uncontrollably.*

SCENE XI

———— ⌾ ————

HE DOES IT WITH JUST
ONE HAND

Music. MERRICK *working on model of St. Phillip's church. Enter* DUCHESS. *At side* TREVES *ticks off a gift list.*

MERRICK: Your grace.

DUCHESS: How nicely the model is coming along, Mr. Merrick. I've come to say Happy Christmas, and that I hope you will enjoy this ring and remember your friend by it.

MERRICK: Your grace, thank you.

DUCHESS: I am very pleased to have made your acquaintance. (*Exits.*)

Enter COUNTESS.

COUNTESS: Please accept these silver-backed brushes and comb for Christmas, Mr. Merrick.

MERRICK: With many thanks, Countess.

COUNTESS: I am very pleased to have made your acquaintance. (*Exits.*)

Enter LORD JOHN.

LORD JOHN: Here's the silver-topped walking stick, Merrick. Make you a regular Piccadilly exquisite. Keep up the good work. Self-help is the best help. Example to us all.

MERRICK: Thank you, Lord John.

LORD JOHN: Very pleased to have made your acquaintance. *(Exits.)*

Enter TREVES *and* PRINCESS ALEXANDRA.

TREVES: Her Royal Highness Princess Alexandra.

PRINCESS: The happiest of Christmases, Mr. Merrick.

TREVES: Her Royal Highness has brought you a signed photograph of herself.

MERRICK: I am honored, your Royal Highness. It is the treasure of my possessions. I have written to His Royal Highness the Prince of Wales to thank him for the pheasants and woodcock he sent.

PRINCESS: You are a credit to Mr. Treves, Mr. Merrick. Mr. Treves, you are a credit to medicine, to England, and to Christendom. I am so very pleased to have made your acquaintance.

PRINCESS, TREVES *exit. Enter* MRS. KENDAL.

MRS. KENDAL: Good news, John. Bertie says we may use the Royal Box whenever I like. Mrs. Keppel says it gives a unique perspective. And for Christmas, ivory-handled razors and toothbrush.

Enter TREVES.

TREVES: And a cigarette case, my boy, full of cigarettes!

MERRICK: Thank you. Very much.

MRS. KENDAL: Look Freddie, look. The model of St. Phillip's.

TREVES: It is remarkable, I know.

MERRICK: And I do it with just one hand, they all say.

MRS. KENDAL: You are an artist, John Merrick, an artist.

MERRICK: I did not begin to build at first. Not till I saw what St. Phillip's really was. It is not stone and steel and glass; it is an imitation of grace flying up and up from the mud. So I make my imitation of an imitation. But even in that is heaven to me, Mrs. Kendal.

TREVES: That thought's got a good line, John. Plato believed this was all a world of illusion and that artists made illusions of illusions of heaven.

MERRICK: You mean we are all just copies? Of originals?

TREVES: That's it.

MERRICK: Who made the copies?

TREVES: God. The Demi-urge.

MERRICK *(goes back to work)*: He should have used both hands shouldn't he?

Music. Puts another piece on St. Phillip's. Fadeout.

SCENE XII

———— ✥ ————

WHO DOES HE REMIND
YOU OF?

TREVES, MRS. KENDAL.

TREVES: Why all those toilet articles, tell me? He is much too deformed to use any of them.

MRS. KENDAL: Props of course. To make himself. As I make me.

TREVES: You? You think of yourself.

MRS. KENDAL: Well. He is gentle, almost feminine. Cheerful, honest within limits, a serious artist in his way. He is almost like me.

Enter BISHOP HOW.

BISHOP: He is religious and devout. He knows salvation must radiate to us or all is lost, which it's certainly not.

Enter GOMM.

GOMM: He seems practical, like me. He has seen enough of daily evil to be thankful for small goods that come

39

his way. He knows what side his bread is buttered on, and counts his blessings for it. Like me.

Enter DUCHESS.

DUCHESS: I can speak with him of anything. For I know he is discreet. Like me.

All exit except TREVES.

TREVES: How odd. I think him curious, compassionate, concerned about the world, well, rather like myself, Freddie Treves, 1889 AD.

Enter MRS. KENDAL.

MRS. KENDAL: Of course he is rather odd. And hurt. And helpless not to show the struggling. And so am I.

Enter GOMM.

GOMM: He knows I use him to raise money for the London, I am certain. He understands I would be derelict if I didn't. He is wary of any promise, yet he fits in well. Like me.

Enter BISHOP HOW.

BISHOP: I as a seminarist had many of the same doubts. Struggled as he does. And hope they may be overcome.

Enter PRINCESS ALEXANDRA.

PRINCESS: When my husband His Royal Highness Edward Prince of Wales asked Dr. Treves to be his personal surgeon, he said, "Dear Freddie, if you can put up with the Elephant bloke, you can surely put up with me."

All exit, except TREVES. *Enter* LORD JOHN.

LORD JOHN: See him out of fashion, Freddie. As he sees me. Social contacts critical. Oh—by the way—ignore the bloody papers; all lies. *(Exits.)*

TREVES: Merrick visibly worse than 86-87. That, as he rises higher in the consolations of society, he gets visibly more grotesque is proof definitive he is like me. Like his condition, which I make no sense of, I make no sense of mine.

Spot on MERRICK *placing another piece on St. Phillip's. Fadeout.*

SCENE XIII

ANXIETIES OF THE SWAMP

MERRICK, *in spot, strains to listen:* TREVES, LORD JOHN *outside.*

TREVES: But the papers are saying you broke the contracts. They are saying you've lost the money.

LORD JOHN: Freddie, if I were such a scoundrel, how would I dare face investors like yourself. Broken contracts! I never considered them actual contracts—just preliminary things, get the old deal under way. An actual contract's something between gentlemen; and this attack on me shows they are no gentlemen. Now I'm only here to say the company remains a terribly attractive proposition. Don't you think? To recapitalize—if you could spare another—ah.

(*Enter* GOMM.)

Mr. Gomm. How good to see you. Just remarking how splendidly Merrick thrives here, thanks to you and Freddie.

GOMM: Lord John. Allow me: I must take Frederick from you. Keep him at work. It's in his contract. Wouldn't

42

want him breaking it. Sort of thing makes the world fly apart, isn't it?

LORD JOHN: Yes. Well. Of course, mmm.

GOMM: Sorry to hear you're so pressed. Expect we'll see less of you around the London now?

LORD JOHN: Of course, I, actually—ah! Overdue actually. Appointment in the City. Freddie. Mr. Gomm. *(Exits.)*

TREVES: He plain fooled me. He was kind to Merrick.

GOMM: You have risen fast and easily, my boy. You've forgot how to protect yourself. Break now.

TREVES: It does not seem right somehow.

GOMM: The man's a moral swamp. Is that not clear yet? Is he attractive? Deceit often is. Friendly? Swindlers can be. Another loan? Not another cent. It may be your money, Freddie; but I will not tolerate laboring like a navvy that the London should represent honest charitable and compassionate science, and have titled swindlers mucking up the pitch. He has succeeded in destroying himself so rabidly, you ought not doubt an instant it was his real aim all along. He broke the contracts, gambled the money away, lied, and like an infant in his mess, gurgles and wants to do it again. Never mind details, don't want to know. Break and be glad. Don't hesitate. Today. One-man moral swamp. Don't be sucked in.

Enter MRS. KENDAL.

MRS. KENDAL: Have you seen the papers?

TREVES: Yes.

GOMM: Yes, yes. A great pity. Freddie: today. (*Exits.*)

MRS. KENDAL: Freddie?

TREVES: He has used us. I shall be all right. Come.

> MRS. KENDAL, TREVES *enter to* MERRICK.

> John: I shall not be able to stay this visit. I must, well, unravel a few things. Nurse Ireland and Snork are—?

MERRICK: Friendly and respectful, Frederick.

TREVES: I'll look in in a few days.

MERRICK: Did I do something wrong?

MRS. KENDAL: No.

TREVES: This is a hospital. Not a marketplace. Don't forget it, ever. Sorry. Not you. Me. *(Exits.)*

MRS. KENDAL: Well. Shall we weave today? Don't you think weaving might be fun? So many things are fun. Most men really can't enjoy them. Their loss, isn't it? I like little activities which engage me; there's something ancient in it, I don't know. Before all this. Would you like to try? John?

MERRICK: Frederick said I may stay here for life.

MRS. KENDAL: And so you shall.

MERRICK: If he is in trouble?

MRS. KENDAL: Frederick is your protector, John.

MERRICK: If he is in trouble? (*He picks up small photo-graph.*)

MRS. KENDAL: Who is that? Ah, is it not your mother? She is pretty, isn't she?

MERRICK: Will Frederick keep his word with me, his contract, Mrs. Kendal? If he is in trouble.

MRS. KENDAL: What? Contract? Did you say?

MERRICK: And will you?

MRS. KENDAL: I? What? Will I?

MERRICK *silent. Puts another piece on model. Fadeout.*

SCENE XIV

ART IS PERMITTED BUT NATURE FORBIDDEN

Rain. MERRICK *working.* MRS. KENDAL.

MERRICK: The Prince has a mistress. *(Silence.)* The Irishman had one. Everyone seems to. Or a wife. Some have both. I have concluded I need a mistress. It is bad enough not to sleep like others.

MRS. KENDAL: Sitting up, you mean. Couldn't be very restful.

MERRICK: I have to. Too heavy to lay down. My head. But to sleep alone; that is worst of all.

MRS. KENDAL: The artist expresses his love through his works. That is civilization.

MERRICK: Are you very shocked?

MRS. KENDAL: Why should I be?

MERRICK: Others would be.

MRS. KENDAL: I am not others.

MERRICK: I suppose it is hopeless.

46

MRS. KENDAL: Nothing is hopeless. However it is unlikely.

MERRICK: I thought you might have a few ideas.

MRS. KENDAL: I can guess who has ideas here.

MERRICK: You don't know something. I have never even seen a naked woman.

MRS. KENDAL: Surely in all the fairs you worked.

MERRICK: I mean a real woman.

MRS. KENDAL: Is one more real than another?

MERRICK: I mean like the ones in the theater. The opera.

MRS. KENDAL: Surely you can't mean they are more real.

MERRICK: In the audience. A woman not worn out early. Not deformed by awful life. A lady. Someone kept up. Respectful of herself. You don't know what fairgrounds are like, Mrs. Kendal.

MRS. KENDAL: You mean someone like Princess Alexandra?

MERRICK: Not so old.

MRS. KENDAL: Ah. Like Dorothy.

MERRICK: She does not look happy. No.

MRS. KENDAL: Lady Ellen?

MERRICK: Too thin.

MRS. KENDAL: Then who?

MERRICK: Certain women. They have a kind of ripeness. They seem to stop at a perfect point.

MRS. KENDAL: My dear she doesn't exist.

MERRICK: That is probably why I never saw her.

MRS. KENDAL: What would your friend Bishop How say of all this I wonder?

MERRICK: He says I should put these things out of my mind.

MRS. KENDAL: Is that the best he can suggest?

MERRICK: I put them out of my mind. They reappeared, snap.

MRS. KENDAL: What about Frederick?

MERRICK: He would be appalled if I told him.

MRS. KENDAL: I am flattered. Too little trust has maimed my life. But that is another story.

MERRICK: What a rain. Are we going to read this afternoon?

MRS. KENDAL: Yes. Some women are lucky to look well, that is all. It is a rather arbitrary gift; it has no really good use, though it has uses, I will say that. Anyway it does not signify very much.

MERRICK: To me it does.

MRS. KENDAL: Well. You are mistaken.

MERRICK: What are we going to read?

MRS. KENDAL: Trust is very important you know. I trust you.

MERRICK: Thank you very much. I have a book of Thomas Hardy's here. He is a friend of Frederick's. Shall we read that?

MRS. KENDAL: Turn around a moment. Don't look.

MERRICK: Is this a game?

MRS. KENDAL: I would not call it a game. A surprise. *(She begins undressing.)*

MERRICK: What kind of a surprise?

MRS. KENDAL: I saw photographs of you. Before I met you. You didn't know that, did you?

MERRICK: The ones from the first time, in '84? No, I didn't.

MRS. KENDAL: I felt it was—unjust. I don't know why. I cannot say my sense of justice is my most highly developed characteristic. You may turn around again. Well. A little funny, isn't it?

MERRICK: It is the most beautiful sight I have seen. Ever.

MRS. KENDAL: If you tell anyone, I shall not see you again, we shall not read, we shall not talk, we shall do nothing. Wait. *(Undoes her hair.)* There. No illusions. Now. Well? What is there to say? "I am extremely pleased to have made your acquaintance?"

Enter TREVES.

TREVES: For God's sakes. What is going on here? What is going on?

49

MRS. KENDAL: For a moment, Paradise, Freddie. *(She begins dressing.)*

TREVES: But—have you no sense of decency? Woman, dress yourself quickly.

(Silence. MERRICK *goes to put another piece on St. Phillip's.)*

Are you not ashamed? Do you know what you are? Don't you know what is forbidden?

Fadeout.

SCENE XV

INGRATITUDE

ROSS *in* MERRICK'*s room.*

ROSS: I come actually to ask your forgiveness.

MERRICK: I found a good home, Ross. I forgave you.

ROSS: I was hoping we could work out a deal. Something new maybe.

MERRICK: No.

ROSS: See, I was counting on it. That you were kind-hearted. Like myself. Some things don't change. Got to put your money on the things that don't, I figure. I figure from what I read about you, you don't change. Dukes, Ladies coming to see you. Ask myself why? Figure it's same as always was. Makes 'em feel good about themselves by comparison. Them things don't change. There but for the grace of. So I figure you're selling the same service as always. To better clientele. Difference now is you ain't charging for it.

MERRICK: You make me sound like a whore.

ROSS: You are. I am. They are. Most are. No disgrace, John.

Disgrace is to be a stupid whore. Give it for free. Not capitalize on the interest in you. Not to have a manager then is stupid.

MERRICK: You see this church. I am building it. The people who visit are friends. Not clients. I am not a dog walking on its hind legs.

ROSS: I was thinking. Charge these people. Pleasure of the Elephant Man's company. Something. Right spirit is everything. Do it in the right spirit, they'd pay happily. I'd take ten percent. I'd be okay with ten percent.

MERRICK: Bad luck's made you daft.

ROSS: I helped you, John. Discovered you. Was that daft? No. Only daftness was being at a goldmine without a shovel. Without proper connections. Like Treves has. What's daft? Ross sows, Treves harvests? It's not fair, is it John? When you think about it. I do think about it. Because I'm old. Got something in my throat. You may have noticed. Something in my lung here too. Something in my belly I guess too. I'm not a heap of health, am I? But I'd do well with ten percent. I don't need more than ten percent. Ten percent'd give me a future slightly better'n a cobblestone. This lot would pay, if you charged in the right spirit. I don't ask much.

MERRICK: They're the cream, Ross. They know it. Man like you tries to make them pay, they'll walk away.

ROSS: I'm talking about doing it in the right spirit.

MERRICK: They are my friends. I'd lose everything. For

you. Ross, you lived your life. You robbed me of forty-eight pounds, nine shillings, tuppence. You left me to die. Be satisfied Ross. You've had enough. You kept me like an animal in darkness. You come back and want to rob me again. Will you not be satisfied? Now I am a man like others, you want me to return?

ROSS: Had a woman yet?

MERRICK: Is that what makes a man?

ROSS: In my time it'd do for a start.

MERRICK: Not what makes this one. Yet I am like others.

ROSS: Then I'm condemned. I got no energy to try nothing new. I may as well go to the dosshouse straight. Die there anyway. Between filthy dosshouse rags. Nothing in the belly but acid. I don't like pain, John. The future gives pain sense. Without a future— *(Pauses.)* Five percent? John?

MERRICK: I'm sorry, Ross. It's just the way things are.

ROSS: By god. Then I am lost.

Fadeout.

SCENE XVI

NO RELIABLE GENERAL ANESTHETIC HAS APPEARED YET

TREVES, *reading, makes notes.* MERRICK *works.*

MERRICK: Frederick—do you believe in heaven? Hell? What about Christ? What about God? I believe in heaven. The Bible promises in heaven the crooked shall be made straight.

TREVES: So did the rack, my boy. So do we all.

MERRICK: You don't believe?

TREVES: I will settle for a reliable general anesthetic at this point. Actually, though—I had a patient once. A woman. Operated on her for—a woman's thing. Used ether to anesthetize. Tricky stuff. Didn't come out of it. Pulse stopped, no vital signs, absolutely moribund. Just a big white dead mackerel. Five minutes later, she fretted back to existence, like a lost explorer with a great scoop of the undiscovered.

MERRICK: She saw heaven?

54

TREVES: Well. I quote her: it was neither heavenly nor hellish. Rather like perambulating in a London fog. People drifted by, but no one spoke. London, mind you. Hell's probably the provinces. She was shocked it wasn't more exotic. But allowed as how had she stayed, and got used to the familiar, so to speak, it did have hints of becoming a kind of bliss. She fled.

MERRICK: If you do not believe—why did you send Mrs. Kendal away?

TREVES: Don't forget. It saved you once. My interference. You know well enough—it was not proper.

MERRICK: How can you tell? If you do not believe?

TREVES: There are still standards we abide by.

MERRICK: They make us happy because they are for our own good.

TREVES: Well. Not always.

MERRICK: Oh.

TREVES: Look, if you are angry, just say so.

MERRICK: Whose standards are they?

TREVES: I am not in the mood for this chipping away at the edges, John.

MERRICK: That do not always make us happy because they are not always for our own good?

TREVES: Everyone's. Well. Mine. Everyone's.

MERRICK: That woman's, that Juliet?

TREVES: Juliet?

MERRICK: Who died, then came back.

TREVES: Oh. I see. Yes. Her standards too.

MERRICK: So.

TREVES: So what?

MERRICK: Did you see her? Naked?

TREVES: When I was operating. Of course—

MERRICK: Oh.

TREVES: Oh what?

MERRICK: Is it okay to see them naked if you cut them up afterwards?

TREVES: Good Lord. I'm a surgeon. That is science.

MERRICK: She died. Mrs. Kendal didn't.

TREVES: Well, she came back too.

MERRICK: And Mrs. Kendal didn't. If you mean that.

TREVES: I am trying to read about anesthetics. There is simply no comparison.

MERRICK: Oh.

TREVES: Science is a different thing. This woman came to me to be. I mean, it is not, well, love, you know.

MERRICK: Is that why you're looking for an anesthetic.

TREVES: It would be a boon to surgery.

MERRICK: Because you don't love them.

TREVES: Love's got nothing to do with surgery.

MERRICK: Do you lose many patients?

TREVES: I—some.

MERRICK: Oh.

TREVES: Oh what? What does it matter? Don't you see? If I love, if any surgeon loves her or any patient or not, what does it matter? And what conceivable difference to you?

MERRICK: Because it is your standards we abide by.

TREVES: For God's sakes. If you are angry, just say it. I won't turn you out. Say it: I am angry. Go on. I am angry. I am angry! I am angry!

MERRICK: I believe in heaven.

TREVES: And it is not okay. If they undress if you cut them up. As you put it. Make me sound like Jack the, Jack the Ripper.

MERRICK: No. You worry about anesthetics.

TREVES: Are you having me on?

MERRICK: You are merciful. I myself am proof. Is it not so? *(Pauses.)* Well? Is it not so?

TREVES: Well. I. About Mrs. Kendal—perhaps I was wrong. I, these days that is, I seem to. Lose my head. Taking too much on perhaps. I do not know—what is in me these days.

MERRICK: Will she come back? Mrs. Kendal?

TREVES: I will talk to her again.

MERRICK: But—will she?

TREVES: No. I don't think so.

MERRICK: Oh.

TREVES: There are other things involved. Very. That is. Other things.

MERRICK: Well. Other things. I want to walk now. Think. Other things. *(Begins to exit. Pauses.)* Why? Why won't she?

Silence. MERRICK *exits.*

TREVES: Because I don't want her here when you die. *(He slumps in chair.)*

Fadeout.

SCENE XVII

CRUELTY IS AS NOTHING TO KINDNESS

TREVES *asleep in chair dreams the following:* MERRICK *and* GOMM *dressed as* ROSS *in foreground.*

MERRICK: If he is merely papier maché and paint, a swindler and a fake—

GOMM: No, no, a genuine Dorset dreamer in a moral swamp. Look—he has so forgot how to protect himself he's gone to sleep.

MERRICK: I must examine him. I would not keep him for long, Mr. Gomm.

GOMM: It would be an inconvenience, Mr. Merrick. He is a mainstay of our institution.

MERRICK: Exactly that brought him to my attention. I am Merrick. Here is my card. I am with the mutations cross the road.

GOMM: Frederick, stand up. You must understand. He is very very valuable. We have invested a great deal in him. He is personal surgeon to the Prince of Wales.

MERRICK: But I only wish to examine him. I had not of course dreamed of changing him.

GOMM: But he is a gentleman and a good man.

MERRICK: Therefore exemplary for study as a cruel or deviant one would not be.

GOMM: Oh very well. Have him back for breakfast time or you feed him. Frederick, stand up. Up you bloody donkey, up!

TREVES, *still asleep, stands up. Fadeout.*

SCENE XVIII

WE ARE DEALING WITH
AN EPIDEMIC

TREVES *asleep.* MERRICK *at lecturn.*

MERRICK: The most striking feature about him, note, is the terrifyingly normal head. This allowed him to lie down normally, and therefore to dream in the exclusive personal manner, without the weight of others' dreams accumulating to break his neck. From the brow projected a normal vision of benevolent enlightenment, what we believe to be a kind of self-mesmerized state. The mouth, deformed by satisfaction at being at the hub of the best of existent worlds, was rendered therefore utterly incapable of self-critical speech, thus of the ability to change. The heart showed signs of worry at this unchanging yet untenable state. The back was horribly stiff from being kept against a wall to face the discontent of a world ordered for his convenience. The surgeon's hands were well-developed and strong, capable of the most delicate carvings-up, for others' own good. Due also to the normal head, the right arm was of enormous power; but, so incapable of the distinction between the assertion of authority and the charitable act of giving, that it was often to be found disgustingly beating others— for their own good. The left arm was slighter and fairer, and may be seen in typical position, hand covering the genitals which were treated as a sullen colony in constant need of restriction, governance, punishment. For their own good. To add a further burden to his trouble, the wretched man when a boy developed a disabling spiritual duality, therefore was unable to feel what others feel, nor reach harmony with them. Please. *(*TREVES *shrugs.)* He would thus be denied all means of escape from those he had tormented.

PINS *enter.*

FIRST PIN: Mr. Merrick. You have shown a profound and unknown disorder to us. You have said when he leaves here, it is for his prior life again. I do not think it ought to be permitted. It is a disgrace. It is a pity and a disgrace. It is an indecency in fact. It may be a danger in ways we do not know. Something ought to be done about it.

MERRICK: We hope in twenty years we will understand enough to put an end to this affliction.

FIRST PIN: Twenty years! Sir, that is unacceptable!

MERRICK: Had we caught it early, it might have been different. But his condition has already spread both East and West. The truth is, I am afraid, we are dealing with an epidemic.

MERRICK *puts another piece on St. Phillip's.* PINS *exit.* TREVES *starts awake. Fadeout.*

62

SCENE XIX

THEY CANNOT MAKE OUT
WHAT HE IS SAYING

MERRICK, BISHOP HOW *in background.* BISHOP *gestures,* MERRICK *on knees.* TREVES *foreground. Enter* GOMM.

GOMM: Still beavering away for Christ?

TREVES: Yes.

GOMM: I got your report. He doesn't know, does he?

TREVES: The Bishop?

GOMM: I meant Merrick.

TREVES: No.

GOMM: I shall be sorry when he dies.

TREVES: It will not be unexpected anyway.

GOMM: He's brought the hospital quite a lot of good repute. Quite a lot of contributions too, for that matter. In fact, I like him; never regretted letting him stay on. Though I didn't imagine he'd last this long.

TREVES: His heart won't sustain him much longer. It may even give out when he gets off his bloody knees with that bloody man.

GOMM: What is it, Freddie? What has gone sour for you?

TREVES: It is just—it is the overarc of things, quite inescapable that as he's achieved greater and greater normality, his condition's edged him closer to the grave. So—a parable of growing up? To become more normal is to die? More accepted to worsen? He—it is just a mockery of everything we live by.

GOMM: Sorry, Freddie. Didn't catch that one.

TREVES: Nothing has gone sour. I do not know.

GOMM: Cheer up, man. You are knighted. Your clients will be kings. Nothing succeeds my boy like success. (*Exits.*)

BISHOP *comes from* MERRICK's *room*.

BISHOP: I find my sessions with him utterly moving, Mr. Treves. He struggles so. I suggested he might like to be confirmed; he leaped at it like a man lost in a desert to an oasis.

TREVES: He is very excited to do what others do if he thinks it is what others do.

BISHOP: Do you cast doubt, sir, on his faith?

TREVES: No, sir, I do not. Yet he makes all of us think he is deeply like ourselves. And yet we're not like each other. I conclude that we have polished him like a mirror, and shout hallelujah when he reflects us to the inch. I have grown sorry for it.

BISHOP: I cannot make out what you're saying. Is something troubling you, Mr. Treves?

TREVES: Corsets. How about corsets? Here is a pamphlet I've written due mostly to the grotesque ailments I've seen caused by corsets. Fashion overrules me, of course. My patients do not unstrap themselves of corsets. Some cannot—you know, I have so little time in the week, I spend Sundays in the poor-wards; to keep up with work. Work being twenty-year-old women who look an abused fifty with worn-outedness; young men with appalling industrial conditions I turn out as soon as possible to return to their labors. Happily most of my patients are not poor. They are middle class. They overeat and drink so grossly, they destroy nature in themselves and all around them so fervidly, they will not last. Higher up, sir, above this middle class, I confront these same—deformities—bulged out by unlimited resources and the ruthlessness of privilege into the most scandalous dissipation yoked to the grossest ignorance and constraint. I counsel against it where I can. I am ignored of course. Then, what, sir, could be troubling me? I am an extremely successful Englishman in a successful and respected England which informs me daily by the way it lives that it wants to die. I am in despair in fact. Science, observation, practice, deduction, having led me to these conclusions, can no longer serve as consolation. I apparently see things others don't.

BISHOP: I do wish I understood you better, sir. But as for consolation, there is in Christ's church consolation.

TREVES: I am sure we were not born for mere consolation.

BISHOP: But look at Mr. Merrick's happy example.

TREVES: Oh yes. You'd like my garden too. My dog, my wife, my daughter, pruned, cropped, pollarded and somewhat stupefied. Very happy examples, all of them. Well. Is it all we know how to finally do with— whatever? Nature? Is it? Rob it? No, not really, not nature I mean. Ourselves really. Myself really. Robbed, that is. You do see of course, can't figure out, really, what else to do with them. Can we? *(Laughs.)*

BISHOP: It is not exactly clear, sir.

TREVES: I am an awfully good gardener. Is that clear? By god I take such good care of anything, anything you, we, are convinced—are you not convinced, him I mean, is not very dangerously human? I mean how could he be? After what we've given him? What you like, sir, is that he is so grateful for patrons, so greedy to be patronized, and no demands, no rights, no hopes; past perverted, present false, future nil. What better could you ask? He puts up with all of it. Of course I do mean taken when I say given, as in what, what, what we have given him, but. You knew that. I'll bet. Because. I. I. I. I—

BISHOP: Do you mean Charity? I cannot tell what you are saying.

TREVES: Help me. *(Weeps.)*

BISHOP *consoles him.*

MERRICK *(rises, puts last piece on St. Phillip's)*: It is done.

Fadeout.

66

SCENE XX

THE WEIGHT OF DREAMS

MERRICK *alone, looking at model. Enter* SNORK *with lunch.*

SNORK: Lunch, Mr. Merrick. I'll set it up. Maybe you'd like a walk after lunch. April's doing wonders for the gardens.

(A funeral procession passes slowly by.)

My mate Will, his sister died yesterday. Twenty-eight she was. Imagine that. Wife was sick, his sister nursed her. Was a real bloom that girl. Now wife okay, sister just ups and dies. It's all so—what's that word? Forgot it. It means chance-y. Well. Forgot it. Chance-y'll do. Have a good lunch. *(Exits.)*

MERRICK *eats a little, breathes on model, polishes it, goes to bed, arms on knees, head on arms, the position in which he must sleep.*

MERRICK: Chancey? *(Sleeps.)*

Enter PINHEADS *singing.*

PINS: We are the Queens of the Cosmos

67

Beautiful darkness' empire
Darkness darkness, light's true flower,
Here is eternity's finest hour
Sleep like others you learn to admire
Be like your mother, be like your sire.

They straighten MERRICK *out to normal sleep position. His head tilts over too far. His arms fly up clawing the air. He dies. As light fades,* SNORK *enters.*

SNORK: I remember it, Mr. Merrick. The word is "arbitrary." Arbitrary. It's all so—oh. Hey! Hey! The Elephant Man is dead!

Fadeout.

SCENE XXI

--------♦♦♦♦--------

FINAL REPORT TO THE
INVESTORS

GOMM *reading,* TREVES *listening.*

GOMM: "To the Editor of the *Times.* Sir; In November,
1886, you were kind enough to insert in the *Times* a
letter from me drawing attention to the case of Joseph
Merrick—"

TREVES: John. John Merrick.

GOMM: Well. "—known as the Elephant Man. It was
one of singular and exceptional misfortune" et cetera et cetera ". . . debarred from earning his liveli-
hood in any other way than being exhibited to the
gaze of the curious. This having been rightly interfered with by the police . . ." et cetera et cetera,
"with great difficulty he succeeded somehow or
other in getting to the door of the London Hospital
where through the kindness of one of our surgeons
he was sheltered for a time." And then . . . and
then . . . and . . . ah. "While deterred by common
humanity from evicting him again into the open
street, I wrote to you and from that moment all

69

difficulty vanished; the sympathy of many was aroused, and although no other fitting refuge was offered, a sufficient sum was placed at my disposal, apart from the funds of the hospital, to maintain him for what did not promise to be a prolonged life. As—"

TREVES: I forgot. The coroner said it was death by asphyxiation. The weight of the head crushed the windpipe.

GOMM: Well. I go on to say about how he spent his time here, that all attempted to alleviate his misery, that he was visited by the highest in the land et cetera, et cetera, that in general he joined our lives as best he could, and: "In spite of all this indulgence, he was quiet and unassuming, grateful for all that was done for him, and conformed readily to the restrictions which were necessary." Will that do so far, do you think?

TREVES: Should think it would.

GOMM: Wouldn't add anything else, would you?

TREVES: Well. He was highly intelligent. He had an acute sensibility; and worst for him, a romantic imagination. No, no. Never mind. I am really not certain of any of it. *(Exits.)*

GOMM: "I have given these details thinking that those who sent money to use for his support would like to know how their charity was used. Last Friday afternoon, though apparently in his usual health, he quietly passed away in his sleep. I have left in my hands a small balance of the money for his support, and this I now propose, after paying certain gratuities, to hand over to the general funds of the hospital. This course I believe will be consonant with the wishes of the contributors.

"It was the courtesy of the *Times* in inserting my letter in 1886 that procured for this afflicted man a comfortable protection during the last years of a previously wretched existence, and I desire to take this opportunity of thankfully acknowledging it.

"I am sir, your obedient servant,
F. C. Carr Gomm
"House Committee Room, London Hospital."
15 April 1890.

TREVES *reenters*.

TREVES: I did think of one small thing.

GOMM: It's too late, I'm afraid. It is done. *(Smiles.)*

Hold before fadeout.

OTHER GROVE PRESS DRAMA
AND THEATER PAPERBACKS

E33   BECKETT, SAMUEL / Waiting for Godot / $1.95 [See also
        Seven Plays of the Modern Theater, Harold Clurman, ed.,
        E 717 / $6.95]
B411   BEHAN, BRENDAN / The Complete Plays (The Hostage, The
        Quare Fellow, Richard's Cork Leg, Three One Act Plays for
        Radio) / $3.95
B79   BEHAN, BRENDAN / The Quare Fellow and The Hostage:
        Two Plays / $2.95 [See also Seven Plays of the Modern
        Theater, Harold Clurman, ed., E717 / $6.95]
E624   BEHAN, BRENDAN / Richard's Cork Leg / $2.95 [See also
        The Complete Plays, Brendan Behan, B411 / $3.95]
E90   BETTI, UGO / Three Plays (The Queen and the Rebels, The
        Burnt Flower-Bed, Summertime) / $3.95
B60   BRECHT, BERTOLT / Baal, A Man's A Man, The Elephant
        Calf / $1.95 [See also Seven Plays by Bertolt Brecht, GP248 /
        $12.50 and The Jewish Wife and Other Short Plays, B80 /
        $1.95]
B312   BRECHT, BERTOLT / The Caucasian Chalk Circle / $1.95
        [See also Seven Plays by Bertolt Brecht, GP248 / $12.50 and
        Grove Press Modern Drama, John Lahr, ed., E633 / $5.95]
B119   BRECHT, BERTOLT / Edward II: A Chronicle Play / $1.45
B120   BRECHT, BERTOLT / Galileo / $1.95 [See also Seven Plays
        by Bertolt Brecht, GP248 / $12.50]
B117   BRECHT, BERTOLT / The Good Woman of Setzuan / $1.95
        [See also Seven Plays by Bertolt Brecht, GP248 / $12.50]
B80   BRECHT, BERTOLT / The Jewish Wife and Other Short Plays
        (In Search of Justice, The Informer, The Elephant Calf, The
        Measures Taken, The Exception and the Rule, Salzburg
        Dance of Death) / $1.95
B89   BRECHT, BERTOLT / The Jungle of Cities and Other Plays
        (Drums in the Night, Roundheads and Peakheads) / $1.95
B129   BRECHT, BERTOLT / Manual of Piety / $2.45
B414   BRECHT, BERTOLT / The Mother / $2.95
B108   BRECHT, BERTOLT / Mother Courage and Her Children /
        $1.95 [See also Seven Plays by Bertolt Brecht, GP248 /
        $12.50]
GP248   BRECHT, BERTOLT / Seven Plays by Bertolt Brecht (In the
        Swamp, A Man's A Man, Saint Joan of the Stockyards, Mother
        Courage and Her Children, Galileo, The Good Woman of
        Setzuan, The Caucasian Chalk Circle) / $12.50
B333   BRECHT, BERTOLT / The Threepenny Opera / $1.95
E517   BULGAKOV, MIKHAIL / Flight: A Play in Eight Dreams and
        Four Acts / $2.25
B193   BULGAKOV, MIKHAIL / Heart of a Dog / $2.95
B147   BULGAKOV, MIKHAIL / The Master and Margarita / $3.95
E693   CHEKHOV, ANTON / The Cherry Orchard / $2.95

E717   CLURMAN, HAROLD, ed. / Seven Plays of the Modern Theater (Waiting for Godot by Samuel Beckett, The Quare Fellow by Brendan Behan, A Taste of Honey by Shelagh Delaney, The Connection by Jack Gelber, The Balcony by Jean Genet, Rhinoceros by Eugene Ionesco, The Birthday Party by Harold Pinter) / $6.95

E159   DELANEY, SHELAGH / A Taste of Honey / $2.95 [See also Seven Plays of the Modern Theater, Harold Clurman, ed., E717 / $6.95]

E380   DURRENMATT, FRIEDRICH / The Physicists / $2.95

E344   DURRENMATT, FRIEDRICH / The Visit / $2.95

B132   GARSON, BARBARA / MacBird! /$1.95

E223   GELBER, JACK / The Connection / $3.95 [See also Seven Plays of the Modern Theater, Harold Clurman, ed., E717 / $6.95]

E130   GENET, JEAN / The Balcony / $2.95 [See also Seven Plays of the Modern Theater, Harold Clurman, ed., E717 / $6.95]

E208   GENET, JEAN / The Blacks: A Clown Show / $2.95 [See also Grove Press Modern Drama, John Lahr, ed., E633 / $5.95]

E577   GENET, JEAN / The Maids and Deathwatch: Two Plays / $3.95

E374   GENET, JEAN / The Screens / $4.95

E677   GRIFFITHS, TREVOR / The Comedians / $3.95

E615   HARRISON, PAUL CARTER, ed. / Kuntu Drama (Great Goodness of Life by Imamu Amiri Baraka, Devil Mas' by Lennox Brown, A Season in the Congo by Aimé Césaire, Mars by Clay Goss, The Great MacDaddy by Paul Carter Harrison, The Owl Answers and A Beast Story by Adrienne Kennedy, Kabnis by Jean Toomer) / $4.95

E457   HERBERT, JOHN / Fortune and Men's Eyes / $3.95

B154   HOCHHUTH, ROLF / The Deputy / $3.95

E456   IONESCO, EUGENE / Exit the King / $2.95

E101   IONESCO, EUGENE / Four Plays (The Bald Soprano, The Lesson, The Chairs, Jack, or The Submission) / $2.95 [See also One Act: Eleven Short Plays of the Modern Theater, Samuel Moon, ed., B107 / $3.95]

E646   IONESCO, EUGENE / A Hell of a Mess / $3.95

E506   IONESCO, EUGENE / Hunger and Thirst and Other Plays (The Picture, Anger, Salutations) / $3.95

E189   IONESCO, EUGENE / The Killer and Other Plays (Improvisation, or The Shepherd's Chameleon, Maid to Marry) / $3.95

E613   IONESCO, EUGENE / Killing Game / $2.95

E614   IONESCO, EUGENE / Macbett / $2.95

E679   IONESCO, EUGENE / Man With Bags / $3.95

E589   IONESCO, EUGENE / Present Past, Past Present / $1.95

E650   NICHOLS, PETER / The National Health / $3.95

B400   ORTON, JOE / The Complete Plays (The Ruffian on the Stair, The Good and Faithful Servant, The Erpingham Camp, Funeral Games, Loot, What the Butler Saw, Entertaining Mr. Sloane) / $4.95

E393   ORTON, JOE / Entertaining Mr. Sloane / $2.95 [See also The Complete Plays of Joe Orton, B400 / $4.95]

E470   ORTON, JOE / Loot / $2.95 [See also The Complete Plays of Joe Orton, B400 / $4.95]

E315   PINTER, HAROLD / The Birthday and The Room: Two Plays / $2.95 [See also Seven Plays of the Modern Theater, Harold Clurman, ed., E717 / $6.95]

E299   PINTER, HAROLD / The Caretaker and The Dumb Waiter: Two Plays / $2.95

B402   PINTER, HAROLD / Complete Works: One (The Birthday Party, The Room, The Dumb Waiter, A Slight Ache, A Night Out, The Black and White, The Examination) / $3.95

B403   PINTER, HAROLD / Complete Works: Two (The Caretaker, Night School, The Dwarfs, The Collection, The Lover, Five Revue Sketches) / $3.95

B410   PINTER, HAROLD / Complete Works: Three (Landscape, Silence, The Basement, Six Revue Sketches, Tea Party [play], Tea Party [short story], Mac) / $3.95

E411   PINTER, HAROLD / The Homecoming / $1.95

E555   PINTER, HAROLD / Landscape and Silence: Two Plays / $3.95 [See also Complete Works: Three by Harold Pinter, B410 / $3.95]

E432   PINTER, HAROLD / The Lover, Tea Party and The Basement / $2.95 [See also Complete Works: Two by Harold Pinter, B403 / $3.95 and Complete Works: Three by Harold Pinter, B410 / $3.95]

GP604 PINTER, HAROLD / Mac (A Memoir) / $4.50 [See also Complete Works: Three by Harold Pinter, B410 / $3.95]

E480   PINTER, HAROLD / A Night Out, Night School, Revue Sketches: Early Plays / $1.95 [See also Complete Works: One by Harold Pinter, B402 / $3.95 and Complete Works: Two by Harold Pinter, B403 / $3.95]

E663   PINTER, HAROLD / No Man's Land / $1.95

E606   PINTER, HAROLD / Old Times / $1.95

E350   PINTER, HAROLD / Three Plays (The Collection, A Slight Ache, The Dwarfs) / $3.95 [See also Complete Works: One by Harold Pinter, B402 / $3.95 and Complete Works: Two by Harold Pinter, B403 / $3.95]

E497   SHAW, ROBERT / The Man in the Glass Booth / $2.95

E635   SHEPARD, SAM / The Tooth of Crime and Geography of a Horse Dreamer: Two Plays / $3.95

E686   STOPPARD, TOM / Albert's Bridge and Other Plays (If You're Glad I'll Be Frank, Artist Descending a Staircase, Where Are They Now? A Separate Peace) / $3.95

E684   STOPPARD, TOM / Dirty Linen and New-Found-Land: Two Plays / $2.95

E586   STOPPARD, TOM / Enter a Free Man / $2.95

E703   STOPPARD, TOM / Every Good Boy Deserves Favor and The Professional Foul: Two Plays / $3.95

E626   STOPPARD, TOM / Jumpers / $2.95

E489   STOPPARD, TOM / The Real Inspector Hound and After Magritte: Two Plays / $3.95

B319   STOPPARD, TOM / Rosencrantz and Guildenstern Are Dead / $1.95

E661   STOPPARD, TOM / Travesties / $1.95

B226   TYNAN, KENNETH / Oh! Calcutta! / $1.95

E708   VAN ITALLIE, JEAN-CLAUDE / America Hurrah and Other Plays (The Serpent, A Fable, The Hunter and the Bird, Almost Like Being) / $5.95

· E414   VIAN, BORIS / The Empire Builders / $2.95

E434   VIAN, BORIS / The Generals' Tea Party / $1.95

E62   WALEY, ARTHUR, tr. and ed. / The No Plays of Japan / $5.95

E519   WOOD, CHARLES / Dingo / $1.95

CRITICAL STUDIES

E127   ARTAUD, ANTONIN / The Theater and Its Double / $3.95

E441   COHN, RUBY, ed. / Casebook on Waiting for Godot / $3.95

E603   HARRISON, PAUL CARTER / The Drama of Nommo: Black Theater in the African Continuum / $2.45

E695   HAYMAN, RONALD / How To Read A Play / $2.95

E387   IONESCO, EUGENE / Notes and Counternotes: Writings on the Theater / $3.95

GROVE PRESS, INC., 196 West Houston St., New York, N.Y. 10014